RODS AND REELS
for coarse fishing

By Ken Whitehead
Illustrated by Russell Birkett

G000124980

WARD LOCK

© Text and illustrations Ward Lock Limited 1989

First published in Great Britain in 1989
by Ward Lock Limited, 8 Clifford Street
London W1X 1RB

Designed by Bob Vickers
Text filmset in Times
by Litho Link Ltd, Welshpool, Powys

Printed and bound in Great Britain

British Library Cataloguing in Publication Data
Whitehead, Ken, *1930 Aug. 10 —*
    Rods and reels for coarse fishing. —
    (Fishing skills pocket book).
    1. Coarse fish. Angling
    I. Title II. Series
    799.1′1

    ISBN 0-7063-6824-X

CONTENTS

Preface   7

PART 1: FISHING RODS   9

Introduction   11

Rod lengths   23

Taper   26

Action   29

Joints   33

Fittings   35
Handles   35
Rings   37

Choosing a rod   39
General-purpose rods   40
Match-fishing rods   41
Leger rods   42
Spinning rods   44
Carp rods   45
Pike rods   46
Poles   46

Looking after rods   48

Rod repairs   51

PART 2: REELS   57

Introduction   59

Choosing a reel   60
Centrepin reels   63
Fixed-spool reels   66
Closed-face reels   69
Multiplying reels   71

Looking after reels   74

Balancing rod and reel   80

Casting techniques   82
Underarm casting   86
Bait casting: the Overhead cast   87

Playing a fish   89

Index   93

PREFACE

For the novice angler, entering a fishing tackle shop early in his career there is before him a vast array of rods of all lengths, colours, sections, with multi-coloured whippings, rod-rings, handles of different lengths in wood, cork, and plastic. In this volume of the series fishing rods are described in terms of materials, construction and action and the kinds of fishing that they are variously designed for.

The reader will learn that the rod chosen must suit the build of its owner and that taper is a vital factor in producing 'action' – how the rod responds in the hands of an angler.

The necessary partner to a rod is a reel and again the choice for the beginner is formidable. The newcomer sees centrepins, fixed-spools both open and closed-face, multipliers all with a wide range of sizes, models and prices. Here, each kind is described and illustrated, with sound advice on the job each one is designed to do.

The author of this series is Ken Whitehead, an all-round fisherman happy with whatever species is found in the water he happens to be fishing. His biggest fish is a pike well in excess of 30 lb and he can include carp in the early 20s among the many entries in his fishing diary. He has come to feel that while the pike's lifestyle includes the taking of live fish, the use of livebaiting is not for him.

Ken is also a keen game fisherman and regularly seeks sewin and salmon in Wales as well as trout fishing on many of the southern counties reservoirs. He is a lone angler who fishes for pleasure, wary of angling politics and distrustful of complicated fishing tackle and over-talkative anglers.

The artist responsible for the clear, no-nonsense black-and-white drawings is 23-year-old Russell Birkett a young graduate with a BA(Hons) degree in Graphic Information and Design from Falmouth. The illustrations in this series are his first major contribution to the field of book illustration and he intends to pursue a career in publishing. He lives in Eastbourne, Sussex.

Len Cacutt, general editor of the series, has been closely concerned with angling publishing in all its forms, having himself written a number of books and compiled and edited angling books, magazines and encyclopedias for the leading publishers, and was Founder Editor of an angling newspaper.

FISHING RODS

Fishing rods	9
Introduction	11
Rod lengths	23
Taper	26
Action	29
Joints	33
Fittings	35
Handles	35
Rings	37
Choosing a rod	39
General-purpose rods	40
Match-fishing rods	41
Leger rods	42
Spinning rods	44
Carp rods	45
Pike rods	46
Poles	46
Looking after rods	48
Rod repairs	51
Index	93

INTRODUCTION: FISHING RODS

There is no such thing as the perfect fishing rod. It can never be made. Every angler who you talk to about rods will eagerly describe to you what in their opinion is the best — but all they are doing is describing the rod which suits *them*. Before you enter a fishing tackle shop to make your choice and buy your first fishing rod you must consider many facts.

First of all there is your particular build. If you are small in stature, a big rod will be cumbersome for you and counter-productive to your fishing; for you it will be awkward. Try to imagine a short person using a long fishing rod and attempting to make a long cast and you will soon see what the problem is. But equally, at the same time a short rod in the hands of a large person can also be a bad investment and prevent the angler from getting the most enjoyment from the sport.

Imagine a 6 ft man using a 5 ft rod to cast with and you can see that he will be wasting energy.

No matter how hard the angler swings the rod, its shortness will be counter-productive to the distance that can be achieved because the leverage will be quite wrong.

There are, however, a few exceptions to this rule and one of them is pole fishing. With these rods, very different from the usual kind, the length of cast is restricted by the length of pole that is being used because the line is attached directly to the pole's tip. To some extent, the second exception is the fly rod, where the weight of line can help influence the distance that can be achieved.

So not only must the rod 'fit' the angler's body, but it must also be capable of coping with the species of fish that are likely to be caught by the angler (1). The somewhat willow-like match-fishing rod with its delicate tip would be completely out of place when being used for pike fishing, where large lures or baits need to be cast, often over a fair distance. Another instance is the rod used for legering, which will naturally be firmer in its action than a general-purpose coarse-fishing rod.

Finally, there is the question of location — where the angler is going to fish. If the fishing is to be on large, open waters, the angler will need a rod capable of casting a bait over considerable distances if the water is to be

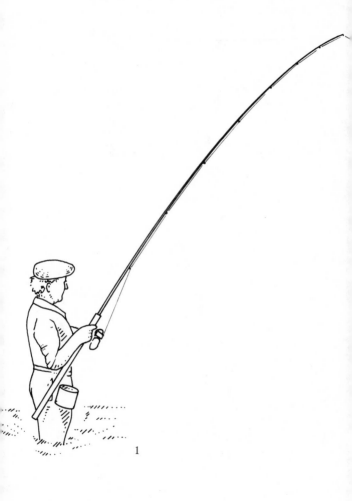

1

explored to find the fish and obtain the best-possible sport from it. (2)

But small waters such as streams, tiny ponds, canals and similar restricted expanses will require a much smaller rod altogether, more especially if there are considerable areas overgrown with trees, bushes and so on that will hinder casting. The kind of water and its surroundings can therefore dictate to some extent the best type of rod.

From time to time tackle manufacturers have tried to introduce on to the market rod designs under the description of combination rods. These models will have several middle and end joints which can be combined in a number of permutations which, in theory at least, provide rods to cope with fish varying in size from a gudgeon weighing an ounce to a 50 lb carp.

But the combination rod has never been a success — principally because when it is in use there is little or no feel to whichever combination of sections the angler has selected. 'Feel' is something that is difficult to describe but can best be summed up as that quality in a rod which allows the angler to sense and possibly predict the moves made by a hooked fish from the vibrations transferred up the line to the rod, and then down to the angler's hand.

Try to imagine how a stout pike-rod would feel if it were playing a minnow, or if a pike were

fighting strongly on a thin and floppy fly rod
and you will get a mental picture of rod feel.
(3)

3

The one-rod-for-different-fish idea is not
workable. This means that the angler is going
to need more than one rod if the wish is to
pursue different species of fish, and this (as
usual these days) will entail some extra
expense. But a word of advice: never try to cut

corners by purchasing cheap fishing rods, or any other fishing gear. Buy a good-quality rod, find out how to use it properly, and study and learn one style of fishing before you move on. Also remember that there are sometimes very good second-hand rods on the market from people who have retired from the sport for some reason. These rods are often very cheap indeed and of excellent quality.

Many different kinds of material have gone into the manufacture of rods over the years, and it is useful to know at least something about all of them — especially if the purchase of a second-hand rod is being considered.

Fishing rods were originally formed from wood, using materials such as whole cane, which was excellent for the butt and middle joints of rods where its hollow centre kept weight to a minimum. Greenheart and lancewood were two other woods used, not just for the whole of the rods but for top joints in both coarse and fly rods. Both of these woods are temperamental and likely to snap or split without warning. They also have a tendency to take up a permanent 'set', or curve, if not stored carefully and in the proper way.

For many years split-cane was the king of rod materials, and it is still sought-after and used today. Six lengths are split from a large-sectioned whole cane and then planed into a tapered v-section, the base part of the triangle being formed from the hard outer surface of the cane. The sections are then glued and fitted together to form the complete rod. The finished article is both tough and sensitive, and the feel of a fish being played on a split-cane rod is unique — but such rods are expensive. Like all woods from which rods are made, cane is delicate and liable to become soft, or take a bend that cannot be removed.

Then came the arrival of rods made from a man-made material, glass-fibre, and this largely superseded the rods made from wood. The first models made from glass-fibre were solid in section, but soon the technique of rolling hollow-section rods on mandrels was perfected and glass-fibre was used for all kinds of fishing rods. But though it was tough, glass-fibre was liable to greenstick-type fractures if excessive pressure or strain was placed upon it. (4)

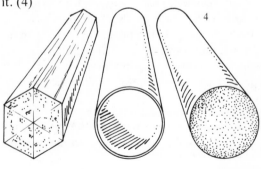

4

Carbon-fibre followed glass-fibre and is now
the most widely used rod-forming material. It
had a few teething problems — largely centred
around its brittleness — but it is now accepted
as probably the best material to date.
Originally very expensive, it has now dropped
greatly in price and rods are available in a
range to suit most pockets. More recently
boron and even more exotic materials have
appeared, but they are expensive and so far
confined almost solely to fly-rod manufacture.

Finally, try to remember the following salient
facts about fishing rods:

- A rod is merely an extension of the angler's
  arm. (5)

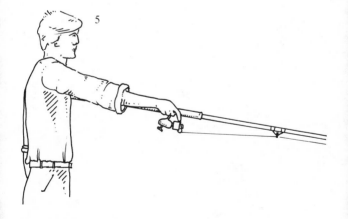

■ It helps you cast the bait towards the fish.
(6)

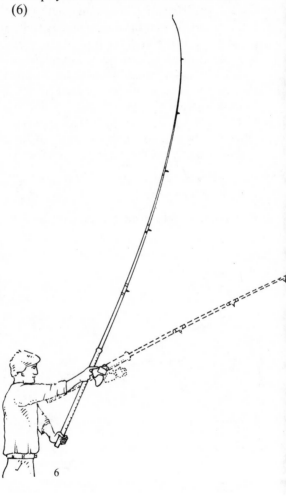

6

■ It helps you make a strike. (7)

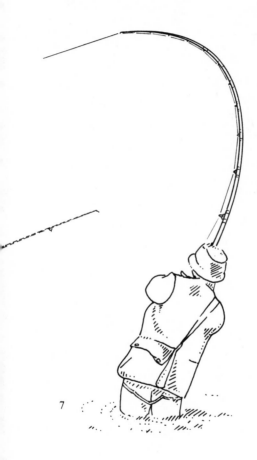

7

■ It helps in playing a fish when it has been hooked. (8)

ROD LENGTHS

The specific job that a rod has been designed to do tends to govern its length and rods fall into some general categories:

- General fishing and match-fishing rods are usually in the 11-13 ft range with three joints. (9)

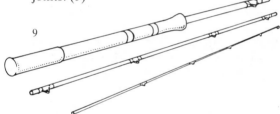

- Legering rods tend to be 9 ft or 9 ft 6 in, using two joints. (10)

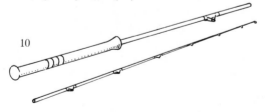

- Spinning rods are in two pieces, either around the 10 ft mark for heavy work, or the 7-9 ft length for lighter casting. (11)

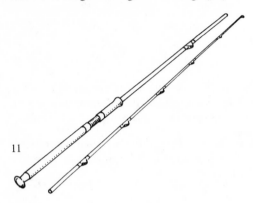

11

- Pike fishing rods used to be 5 ft but now are 10 to 11 ft, similar to spinning rods but with a different action. (12)

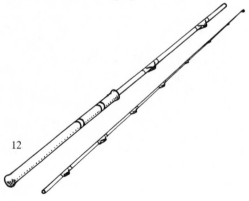

12

■ Roach poles vary in length from 15 to 30 ft,
sometimes even to 40 ft, and can either be
telescopic or be composed of take-apart
joints. (13)

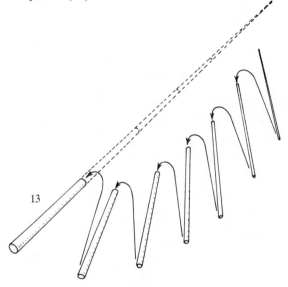

13

ROD TAPER

The way that a rod tapers from its butt to the tip will affect its casting action, the weight that it can cast, and the manner in which it will play a fish. Taper is not just confined to the tip of a rod — the taper in a rod's lower joints is equally important and will affect its overall performance.

- A taper that slowly develops from the butt end of the rod to its tip will be capable of 'springing', or casting, a bait over a considerable distance without it snatching, or breaking free. Such rods are used where heavy baits or tackle need to be used. Spinning rods usually fall in this category. (14)

14

■ Taper that commences mainly in the top
joint will produce a rod with tip action, used
for flicking baits over short distances. Some
general coarse-fishing and most match-
fishing rods tend to fall in this
section. (15)

15

■ Some rods are available with what is called
a reverse taper. Here the taper starts at the
butt end and increases up the rod, then
tapers away towards the tip. The advantage
of this is in increasing the 'spring' imparted
to the bait when it is cast. Usually these
rods are used for sea fishing and for
pike. (16)

16

- Some match-fishing rods work on the fast-taper principle. Here the taper moves in steps through the length of the rod, making for an action that is very much in the tip — ideal for the fast casting and striking that the matchman requires. (17)

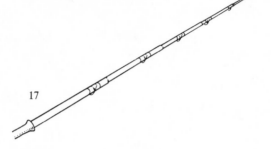

17

ROD ACTION

Naturally, the length of the rod and the taper
that it has been given will produce an action
that is applicable to that rod alone. Some
examples are:

- A long, light rod with a slow taper, which
  will have a soft action. (18)

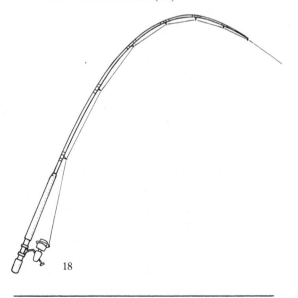

18

- A short rod with little taper in the bottom
  joints but a steep taper in the top joint will
  have what is called a tip action. (19)

19

(To help generalise in the description of rod
action, tackle manufacturers have adopted
two standards. One applies to coarse fishing
rods, the other to rods used for game (fly)
fishing.)

- Coarse fishing rods have their action
  measured by means of a test curve. A simple
  way to understand this is to tie a length of
  line to the tip ring of the rod, and attach this
  to the hook on a spring balance. The rod is
  held vertical and the spring balance pulled
  sideways until the tip of the rod is bent to an
  angle of 90 degrees. At this angle the weight
  is read from the balance, and the reading
  used to describe the rod action. This might
  vary from a few ounces (a light rod) to 1½
  lb. (20)

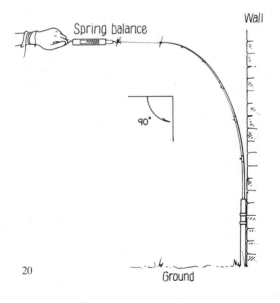

31

- The Association of Fishing Tackle Manufacturers (AFTM) measures action in rods used for fly fishing by the number-sign #. This number refers to the weight of line that will best work with the rod and from it comes a simple guide. Generally #4 to 6 rods are for light work — streams and so on, #7 and 8 for general river and light reservoir work, and #9 and above for work that involves heavy duty casting such as handling heavy weighted fly lines for reservoir or salmon fishing on big rivers. (21)

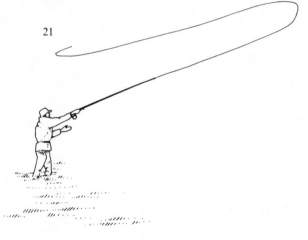

21

ROD JOINTS

The sections of wooden rods are fastened
together by the use of brass fittings called
ferrules, named (for obvious reasons) male
and female, to either end of each joint.
Occasionally they are found in rods made from
solid glass-fibre. (22)

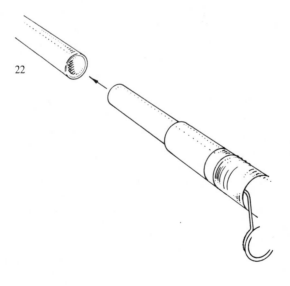

22

■ Hollow-glass and carbon-fibre rods are
connected by spigots, which are formed by
a solid tubular spigot fixed to form the male
mounting at one joint end, into which the
hollow end of the joint above can slide.
Strong and light, these joints rarely give
trouble. (23)

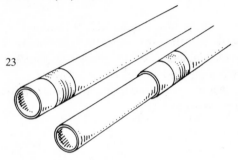

23

ROD FITTINGS

The two essential fittings to a rod are its handle, and the rod rings which guide and control the line. Both are important items and their position and style will influence the action of the rod.

Handles

- Rod handles are either single (short) or double (long) handed. Single-handed rods are usually found on fly rods, and short rods used for spinning. (24)

24

- Double handles are used on longer rods, the extra length of handle providing comfort besides the leverage that assists in developing the cast and in playing a fish. (25)

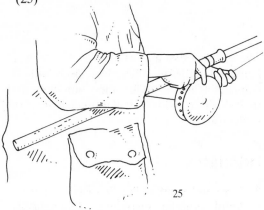

25

- Handles are either formed from cork, wood or plastic. Whichever material forms the handle of your rod, keep it clean and free of slime and grease by using a little liquid soap on a clean cloth when you get home. (26)

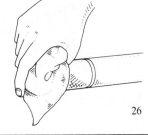

26

Rod Rings

■ For float fishing, rod rings are usually of the
'stand off' type, the rings soldered to tall
legs that will hold the line away from the
rod. This is important — especially when
rain tends to make nylon line cling to the
rod's surface. The best rings are
manufactured from stainless steel, and are
either of satin chrome or black chrome to
prevent glare. (27)

27

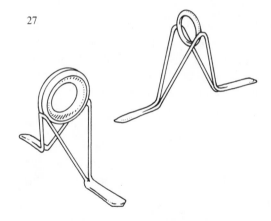

■ Rings for rods that have to cope with heavy
and powerful fish such as carp and pike,
and spinning rods, have heavier rings,
generally lined with a material that will not
wear and form grooves as the line constantly
passes through them. Quality is always

something you will have to pay for — the
price will be reflected in the rod. (28)

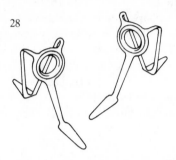

- Butt and end rings — the first and last rings
  on the rod — take the most wear. On good-
  quality rods these will have lined rings, and
  the tip ring will possess legs on either side to
  prevent line wrapping round and jamming.
  (29)

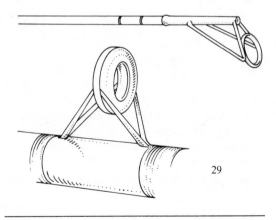

CHOOSING A ROD

Before you commit yourself to parting with
money for a rod, try to borrow one from a
friend. By trying a variety of rods in different
angling situations you will soon decide what
you like, and dislike. (30) Keep in mind that
there is no such thing as an all-round rod —
decide what fish you are going to try to catch
and look for a rod that will cope with those
species. A match-fishing rod is of little use on
a fast river like the Hampshire Avon where
large fish are going to require some firm

30

handling. Conversely, a stiff, general-purpose rod will be the wrong one if you intend to take up match-fishing. When you are in the tackle shop, look carefully at the quality and finish of the rods. A dark model with matt finish, quality rod rings and a well-finished handle will look and fish like a thoroughbred. Those with chrome strips, flash whippings and garish-coloured joints are designed to attract the angler; they will soon lose their shine.

■ **General-purpose float rods.** These have a slow action that produces a bend through a great deal of their length. They will cope with lines up to 5 lb or so in breaking strain, and can handle most situations from long-trotting for chub to tench and light carp fishing. They possess sliding winch fittings that push together over the reel saddle and hold it in place. (31)

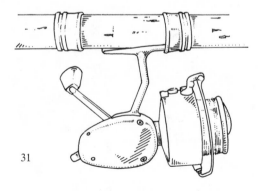

31

- **Match-fishing rods.** These are fast-
  actioned, the taper occurring only in the
  end 25 per cent of the rod which allows for
  objective casting and fast striking on a bite.
  As with general-purpose float rods they are
  equipped with sliding winch fittings. (32)

32

■ **Leger rods.** Shorter — 9 to 9 ft 6 in —
these rods have a moderate action allowing
some firm casting but they retain sensitivity
which will enable a bite to be seen by the
angler. To aid this the rod's tip-ring will be
fitted with the means of using a swingtip,
springtip or quivertip. (33, 34, 35)
Swingtips are aids to detecting a bite and
are screwed into the top ring of the rod or
fastened to a spigot by a piece of valve
rubber. The swingtip is best used on
stillwaters where there is no flow and is
most successful when it hangs at an angle of
90 degrees. *Springtips* have a coiled spring
and wire to register bites. *Quivertips* are
short, stiff extensions which screw into the

Leger rod in action

33

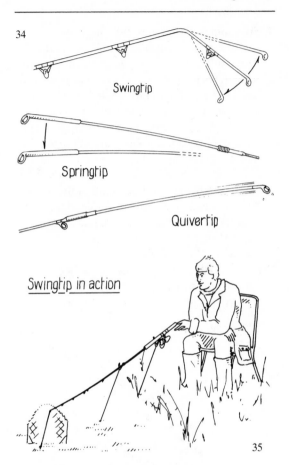

34

Swingtip

Springtip

Quivertip

Swingtip in action

35

end ring of the rod, and register the slightest
move from a fish. Painted with bright
colours they are very effective when used
on moving waters.

■ **Spinning rods.** These fall into two
categories — single and double handed.
The double-handed rod will be from 9 to 10
ft long, with a test curve of 1½ to 2¼ lb, and
possess a slow action which will enable it to
handle sizable baits. The reel fittings will be
screw actioned, allowing the reel to be
clamped firmly to the butt, unable to work
free with the constant casting that will take
place. Single-handed spinning rods, used on
small waters or from boats, are in the 6 to 8
ft range (36). Originally introduced into this
country from the US they are known as
baitcasting rods, and are designed to be
used with a multiplying reel. To help control
the line, a true baitcasting rod has a cranked
handle into which the reel clips. With this
feature it is possible to cast continuously

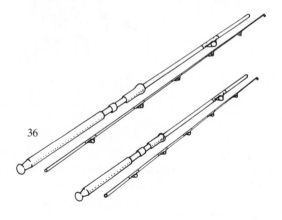

36

and without fatigue throughout the day, allowing the angler to cover a lot of water. (37)

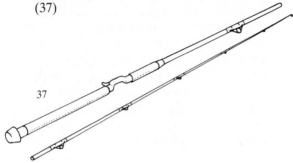

37

■ **Carp rods.** There are many special rods on the market, some of which have been designed by famous anglers and which are capable of handling very large carp. They tend to be in the 11 ft range with a test curve of 1½ lb, handling a line of 6-12 lb breaking strain and are capable of making long casts that are often necessary to get a bait to the fish. (38)

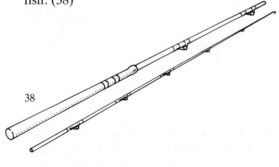

38

■ **Pike rods.** These operate best when they have fast-taper blanks with a test curve in the 2¼ to 2½ lb range and when the angler is using small baits. But for long-range casting with heavy baits a slow-action rod will be better. There are many specialist pike rods sporting well known names in the tackle shops. Some anglers have been known to use light sea fishing beachcasters on very large waters, where baits have to be cast over a long distance. (39)

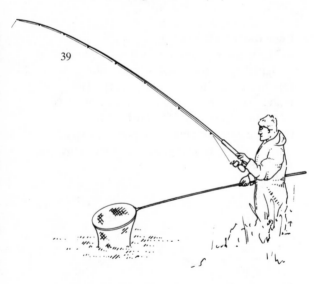

39

■ **Poles.** Originally made from hollow cane and used exclusively on the Thames and Lea for roach, the pole is now one of the chief weapons in the match-angler's armoury and is used on waters throughout the country and on the Continent. Generally poles vary in length from 15 to 30 ft, and the more you pay then the better they are. For the best poles you can pay up to £1,000. Their advantage is that they enable complete line control and keep the rod tip on top of the float, ready to deal with the most sensitive of bites. The alloy crook and length of elastic allow some give in playing a fish — quite a big consideration when there is no reel, the line being attached to the top of the rod. (40, 41)

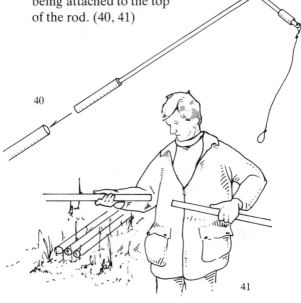

40

41

LOOKING AFTER RODS

Rods never wear out. The rings may become worn, and the varnish scuffed — but rods usually fail because they have been neglected or damaged in some way. One of the first things to remember is that a rod must be kept in its case, which will keep all the joints together. To keep them safely when not in use they should be hung by the loop at the bag end in the dry. (42)

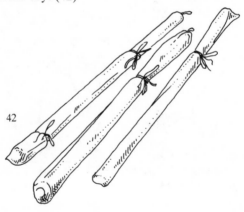

42

■ After use, wipe and dry your rods when you get home. Damp working its way under the rod whippings is one of the quickest ways of losing a rod ring — just at the wrong moment. (43)

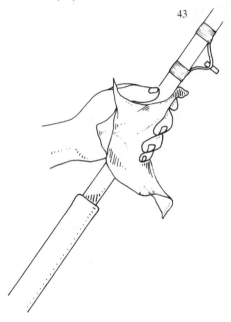

43

■ Pay special attention to the handle. Clean it with a little washing-up liquid and rinse and dry thoroughly.

- When going fishing it pays to carry your rods in a holdall, which not only keeps them together but also gives added protection against knocks. Several types are on the market, either as tubes or roll-up models. Choose one large enough to take an umbrella as well. (44)

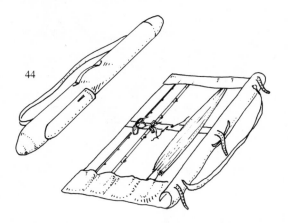

44

ROD REPAIRS

There is not much that can go wrong with the modern fishing rod, but there are two areas of wear that will occur and which will need attention. But don't panic, these are well within the angler's grasp.

- When spigots wear, the ends of the two joints butt together. This will loosen them and the rod joint will separate when you cast. The cure is to take a medium file and gently remove a little from off the female joint end. (45)

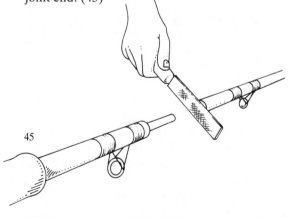

45

- Carry out the filing a little at a time and constantly check the fit. If you take too much off, the joints won't fit together, and if you have planned a fishing trip for the next day you will have a problem.

- Damaged rod whippings (sometimes called wrappings) should be repaired as soon as possible. Your tackle dealer will be able to sell you a reel of whipping material to match that which needs replacing. You will also need cellulose varnish and some ordinary rod varnish — also available at the tackle dealer. (46)

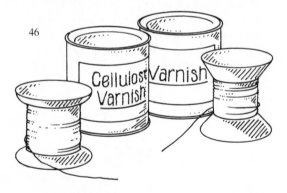

46

- Start by removing the ring from the rod and cleaning off old varnish and whipping and gently rubbing the area with extra fine glass paper until it is smooth. Then use sticky tape to hold the ring in place. (47)

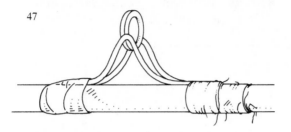

47

■ Trap one end of the whipping by taking a
full turn round the rod below the platform
of the rod ring, then commence winding it
on, keeping each turn tight against the next
one. (48)

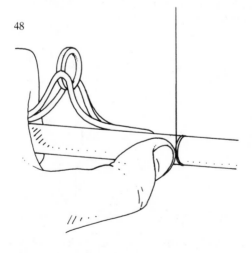

48

■ Carry on until you are within 9 or 10 turns
of the ring legs. (49)

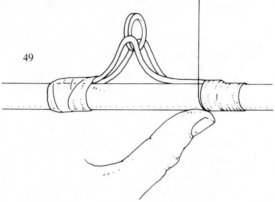

49

■ Then fold a short length of thread and carry
on whipping over this. (50)

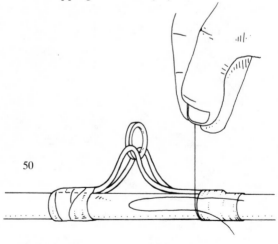

50

■ Thread the whipping end through the loop, and pull it back till it lies under the whipping. (51)

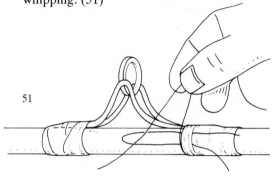

51

■ Hold the end free, and cut with a razor blade. (52)

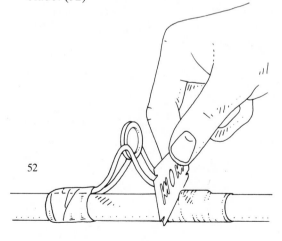

52

■ Flood the whipping with several coats of cellulose varnish until the grooves between the whippings are filled. (53)

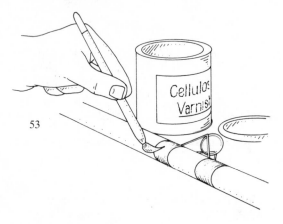

■ When dry, give two coats of rod varnish, leaving to dry in a dust-free place and the job is done. (54)

REELS

Reels	57
Introduction	59
Choosing a reel	60
Centrepin reels	63
Fixed-spool reels	66
Closed-face reels	69
Multiplying reels	71
Looking after reels	74
Balancing rod and reel	80
Casting techniques	82
Underarm casting	86
Bait casting: the Overhead cast	87
Playing a fish	89
Index	93

INTRODUCTION: REELS

Put into simple terms, a reel exists merely to store line without it tangling until the angler is ready to release it, or to retrieve it. No matter how many levers or gears a reel has it can carry out nothing other than these two operations and there is no guarantee that reels which are designed to have several different types of control over the line are any better than the more simple models. (55)

55

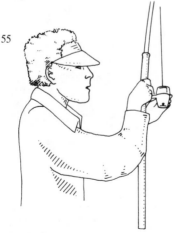

CHOOSING A REEL

The most important thing to look for when selecting a reel is the material from which it has been made, together with the degree of engineering skill and technique that has gone into its design and manufacture. Soft metal, poorly engineered gears and badly sited handles or control levers will make using the reel a nightmare instead of the natural aid that it should be. (56)

56

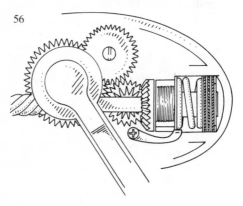

Parting with good money usually ensures that the reel has been made from good-quality metal or, more recently, carbon fibre. It will give a life-time of service — providing that it is looked after. As with selecting a rod, the angler should be careful when he makes his choice of fishing reel. It is essential that the reel should suit the type of fishing to be undertaken, the type of water where it is to be fished, and the species of fish that are to be sought.

Further, the angler must consider that the reel must match the rod he is going to use. This matching together of rod and reel, called balance, is all-important. It is not just size that matters — weight must also be taken into consideration, especially if, for instance, the angler is going to spin — something that will necessitate his holding the rod and casting for most of the day. (57)

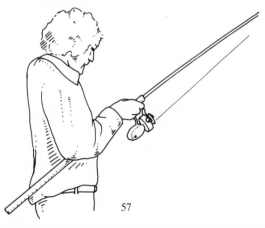

57

There are three types of reel from which the angler can choose, the centrepin reel, the fixed-spool reel and the multiplying reel. Each have their merits and their uses. Before purchasing either of the basic types, try to use one belonging to a friend. (58)

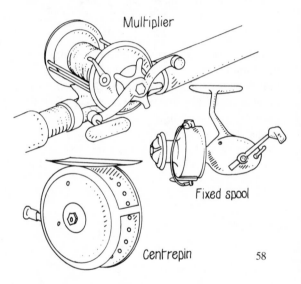

Multiplier

Fixed spool

Centrepin   58

Some reels can be difficult to cope with — for instance, many anglers never manage to get the hang of using a multiplying reel. Persevere and practise — but if you cannot become accustomed to using a particular type of reel, leave it alone. Above all — never just buy a reel simply for its appearance.

CENTREPIN REELS

Basically, a centrepin is a flanged drum which revolves in a close fitting backplate, and the centrepin reel has been in use since anglers needed to store line. The drum revolves in parallel with the rod handle, line feeding directly from the drum into the first rod ring.

- With no angles for the line to follow, this leads to great control and sensitivity. Easy to maintain, the best centrepins cost money — you are paying for the machining of both drum and body — but with only one moving part, there is little wear and a reel will last a lifetime. The principal use of the centrepin is for long-trotting, the current of the river taking float and bait downstream and pulling line straight from the drum while allowing the angler to concentrate on possible bites. Naturally this free-running action is only possible from reels made of light alloy — wooden reels (often called Nottingham reels) and some old Bakelite or plastic ones have a drum too heavy to be moved by the end tackle. Some centrepin models have a drag system fitted which

prevents line being stripped so quickly that
the reel over-runs, causing what is called a
'bird's nest' around the drum. Usually there
is a check that can be switched over by
means of a lever — something useful when
playing a fish. (59)

59

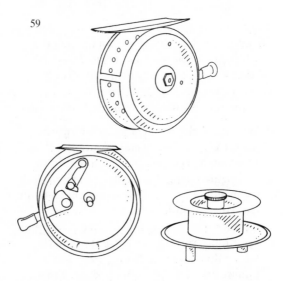

■ Because the reel is so free-running there is
no need to wind line back onto the drum by
the handles on the side of the case. Instead
the line is 'batted' by tapping with the
fingers on the rim of the drum. The careful
positioning of the thumb prevents an
overrun on the retrieve. (60)

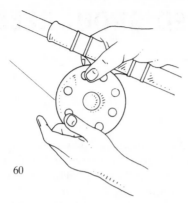

60

■ Out of favour for a number of years, the
centrepin is making a comeback with many
anglers — especially the matchmen — who
appreciate the direct control between reel,
line and fish, without the gears and springs
that are used on other models. When filling
the reel the line is wound onto the spool
directly, using some tension – it is better
that someone holds the spooled line
otherwise line trapping will occur on the
drum. (61)

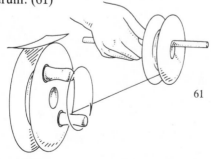

61

FIXED-SPOOL REELS

Originally called threadline reels — so-named
because they used ordinary sewing thread as
line — fixed-spool reels have been one of the
many revolutions in the angling world. With
the aid of a fixed-spool reel it is possible to
cast over considerable distances effortlessly,
and without line tangle.

■ This largely relates to the fact that the drum
of the reel is at right angles to the rod handle
and line is pulled free over the lip of the
reel. The drum does not revolve, as in the
centrepin model. (62)

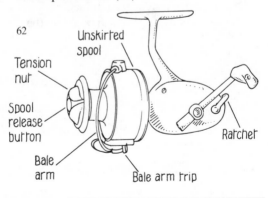

62

Unskirted
spool

Tension
nut

Spool
release
button

Bale
arm

Bale arm trip

Ratchet

■ Another advantage of the fixed-spool reel is that the angler has a clutch between the handle and spool, allowing the line to slip when excessive pull takes place — i.e., when playing a strong-fighting fish. This clutch can be adjusted by using the tension nut usually placed at the front of the reel, in front of the drum. There are, however, models where the drag adjustment is by means of a knob placed behind the body of the reel; an advantage of this positioning is the fact that tension can be adjusted while a fish is being played.

The first fixed-spool reels had an unskirted spool, which allowed line to slip to the rear of the back of the spool and catch on the spindle behind. To avoid this the skirted spool was designed to overcome this difficulty. (63)

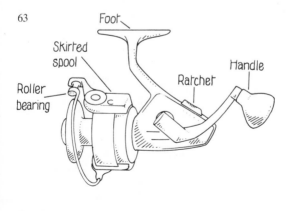

63

Foot

Skirted spool

Handle

Roller bearing

Ratchet

Different gearing on the reel will offer varying rates of retrieve. The normal ratio is 4 to 1, providing a retrieve rate of about 16 in to one turn of the handle.

Line snagging is a problem with any reel — especially when it is windy, or the angler is fishing from banks that are obstructed with undergrowth. To deal with this problem, the tackle manufacturers' designed the closed-face reel.

CLOSED-FACE REELS

Here all mechanism, such as the bale arm around which line fits, is completely covered by a shield. Line is released by pressing a button at the front of the spool, and it will begin retrieval on the first rotation of the handle. The clutch is adjusted by means of a tension knob fitted to the handle, at the junction with the spool. (64)

64

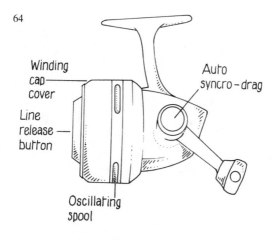

Winding
cap
cover

Line
release
button

Auto
syncro-drag

Oscillating
spool

■ These reels are only as good as the
engineering in them — so you should buy
the best you can afford. There is an inbuilt
disadvantage with the fixed-spool reel, and
that is line twist or kink. Care must be taken
when loading the spool. The revolving
action of the bale arm around the spool puts
a kink into a line being wound directly onto
it — the normal method. Instead, the spool
from which line is drawn should be held
parallel to the drum of the reel, and line
drawn off over its lip, in the same manner
that line leaves the reel during a cast. Take
care to fill the spool with line to within ⅛ of
an inch of the lip. If this is not done, drag
will occur as line is pulled over the lip, and
the length of the line will be restricted. (65,
66)

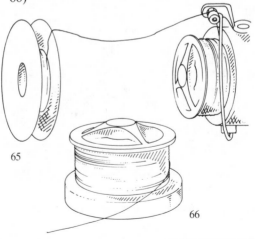

65

66

MULTIPLYING REELS

Multiplying reels, or 'multipliers', are reels that possess a small-diameter drum geared to a ratio of 3 or 4 to 1, so producing a very rapid retrieve of the line. There is a wide variety of this kind of reel on the market, some of the up-to-date models possessing magnetic drags, oil drag retarders and automatic gearing.

- A good multiplier will have centrifugal braking — as the cast progresses so friction pads will slow the drum to prevent over-run. There will also be an automatic line spreader to prevent line piling on one area of the spool, thereby trapping it. (67)

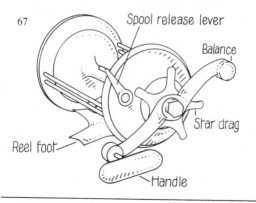

67

Spool release lever

Balance

Star drag

Reel foot

Handle

■ Multiplying reels are different in that they
are fished with the reel above the rod handle
and not below, in the traditional position.
These reels are capable of allowing a sizable
bait to be punched out for a very long
distance, and coping with big fish —
principally through the direct line taken
from reel to rod tip. This is unlike the fixed-
spool reel where line goes at an angle
through the bale arm, then back through
the angle of the butt ring. Line is loaded
onto the spool of the multiplier directly, in
the same way as the centrepin reel. (68)

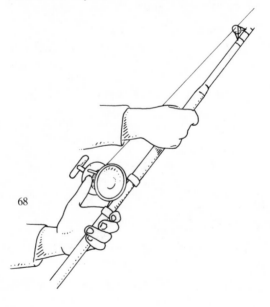

68

- The disadvantages of the multiplying reel lie in their vulnerability to grit and dirt — this can jam them or damage the delicate mechanism inside the end plates — and in unskilled hands they have a tendency to encounter over-runs that produce massive birds' nests. Those anglers who have mastered them swear by them — those who don't, swear at them. The best are expensive but with care they will last a lifetime.

LOOKING AFTER REELS

Dirt, dust and pieces of the angler's bait are a reel's worst enemies. When you buy your reel buy a reel case for it at the same time — there are several varieties on the market, made in sizes to suit every reel. When not in use, keep the reel cased. (69)

69

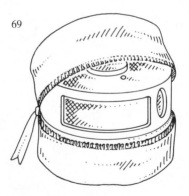

- When you return from a fishing trip, take your reels from their cases and let the cases dry thoroughly. Dry the reel too and then strip it down, removing the drum/spool from the body and cleaning with a dry cloth. (70)

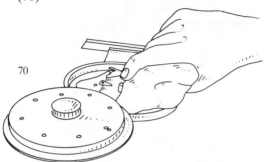

■ Reels for freshwater fishing that have been used in salt or brackish water should immediately be washed in fresh water, then dried. Some metals used in freshwater-reel manufacture will corrode quickly if salt is left adhering. (71)

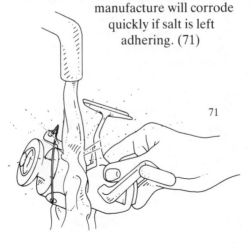

- When dry, wipe the reel body and spool back with a cloth on which a little oil (WD 40 or similar) has been sprayed. Then pack the reel in its case ready for use again. Be careful not to get oil on any monofilament line. (72)

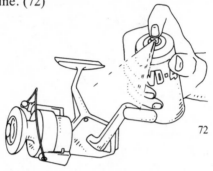

72

- At least once during a season — more with constant use — reels should be completely stripped and oiled or greased. This is especially important in the case of fixed-spool and multiplying reels. (73)

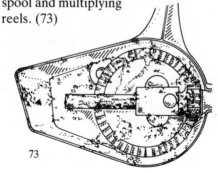

73

■ Brush and work Swarfega or any similar
recommended grease-remover into the body
of the reel with a brush to dissolve stale
grease and dirt. (74)

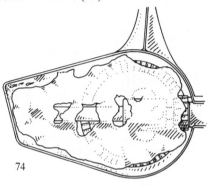

■ Wash under a tap and dry. (75)

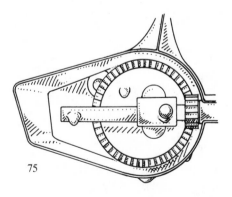

■ Re-pack with grease — your tackle shop
will sell the right type for your reel. (76)

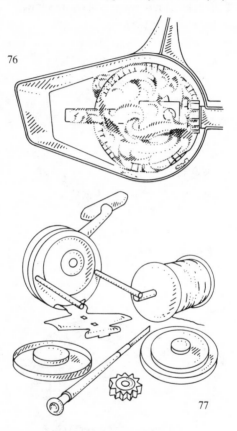

76

77

■ Take special care when dealing with
multiplying reels. Study the manufacturer's
guide before stripping — and do the job on

a table laid with white paper as a background. There are often tiny springs, screws and so on in these reels which can easily be lost. Take special care to use the lubricant recommended by the manufacturer when re-assembling. (77)

- Avoid packing line tightly onto a reel. Each time you get snagged and pull to get free, line with be pulled hard and tight onto the reel, so tightening into the line already stored. If you repeat this several times during an outing, pressure can be caused that will jam folds of line one under the other or, worse, the spool may be distorted and unable to revolve. Always pull line above the tip ring to free a snag, wrapping it round your clothed forearm (not a finger) and taking a straight strain. (78)

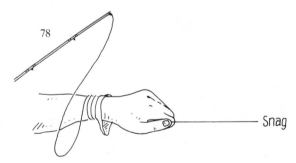

Snag

BALANCING ROD AND REEL

Balance is all important when rod and reel are joined together. Imagine holding something that is either tip heavy or butt heavy for around eight hours and you will get some idea of how tiring and unpleasant it can be. (79)

79

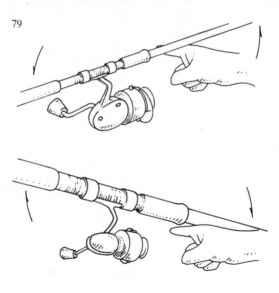

Ideally both reel and rod should balance.
The point of balance is taken as just above
the handle and it is worth going to great
lengths to achieve this when putting rod and
reel together. (80)

80

CASTING TECHNIQUES

Even the best-balanced rod and reel need some know-how from the angler if they are to get the bait where it is wanted. Casting comes with practice, but there is no need to practise at the waterside. Without a hook, casting can be practised in a field and those determined to reach the top in angling — especially match anglers — are not frightened to do so. There are several types of cast, the most universally used in bottom fishing being the overhead cast. The following sequence shows how it may be done.

- Space your hands well apart on the rod handle and keep the rod tip vertical with the float hanging a few feet or so below the tip ring. (81)

- Move the rod backwards over the shoulder until the tip is angled at about 45 degrees. (82)

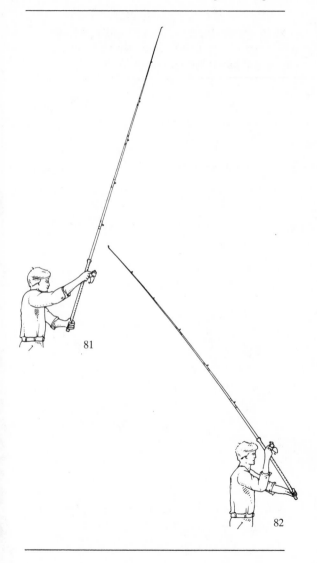

81

82

- Begin the forward stroke boldly pulling
  with the top hand and pulling backwards
  with that at the bottom. (83)

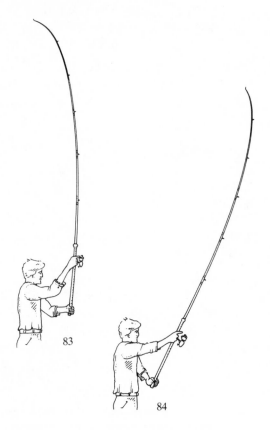

- With the rod around 45 degrees in front of
  you, release line from the reel — (84)

- and hold the rod down, allowing the line to follow through as the bait and float are taken away. (85)

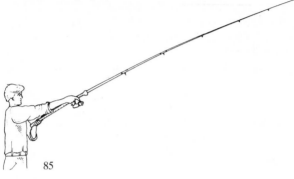

85

- When the bait hits the water keep the rod tip down, and above the surface of the water. (86)

86

Underarm Casting

■ The rod is held in front of the angler, line above the hook in one hand and the finger of the other hand braking the reel, preventing line pulling free. (87)

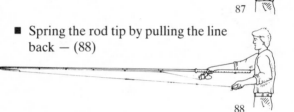

87

■ Spring the rod tip by pulling the line back — (88)

88

■ and release it, swinging the rod up and away so that the bait and float shoot out over the water. (89, 90)

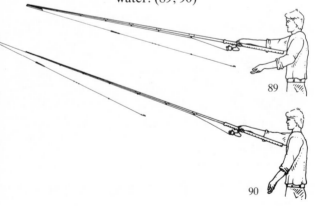

89

90

Bait Casting — The Overhead Cast

- A technique for those spinning with the single handed rod.

- Swing the bait up and backwards over your head. (91)

- Allow the weight of the bait to flex the rod back — (92)

■ then force the rod tip forward, throwing the
  bait forward. (93)

93

■ Keep the rod tip down to allow line to
  follow through. (94)

94

PLAYING A FISH

When a sizable fish is hooked remember that cool and determined action will bring it to the net. Snatching in a panic will surely lose anything but the smallest tiddler. (95)

95

■ While the fish is running and in safe water, i.e. without snags, the fish can have its head — but with resistance from the angler either from the drag on a fixed-spool reel or on the rim of the drum on a centrepin reel. (96)

96

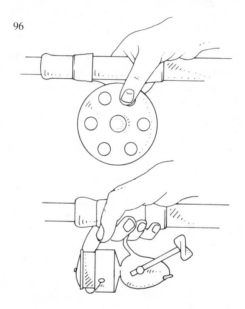

■ When the fish runs into possible cover such as weed beds or overhanging bushes where a break may occur, use side strain to turn its head and alter its direction. Never point the rod towards the fish; keep it at an angle which will allow the spring in the rod to help tire the catch out. (97)

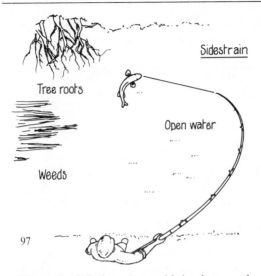

Sidestrain

Tree roots

Open water

Weeds

97

- When the fish tires, 'pump' it back towards you by alternately raising the rod tip and recovering line until it is within range of the landing net. (98)

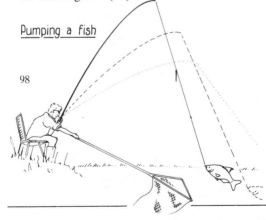

Pumping a fish

98

- Sink the net and draw the fish gently over it. (99)

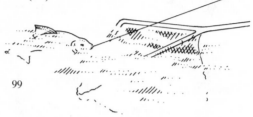

99

- Lift rod and landing net together when the fish is well enveloped, and take it well back up the bank, away from the water. One last tip: always unhook your fish while it is still in the net. If you remove it from the meshes before unhooking it might give a sudden jump and be away, and it might have been that very good specimen you have been trying for for ages! (100)

100

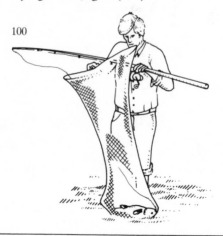

INDEX

Alloy crook (for pole fishing) 47
Automatic line spreader (reels) 71

Bait casting 67
Bait-casting rods 44
Balancing rod and steel 61, 80
Bale-arm (reels) 69, 70
Batting (of reel drum) 64
Blanks (rods) 47
Boron 19
Breaking strain (line) 40

Carbon-fibre 19, 34
Care of reels 74
Carp rods 45
Casting 26, 66, 82
    bait-casting 67
    overhead 82, 87
    underarm 86
Cellulose varnish (for whippings) 52
Centrepin reels 62, 63, 65, 72, 90
Closed-face reels 69
Coarse-fishing rods 30, 31

Combination rods 15
Cork handles 36
Cranked handles (rods) 44

Double-handed rods 44
Drums (reels) 63, 71

Elastic (for pole fishing) 47

Fast taper 28, 46
Ferrules 33
    female 33
    male 33
Fibre-glass (see Glassfibre)
Fixed-spool reels 62, 66, 76, 90
Fly rods 12, 16, 19, 30, 35
Friction pads (reels) 41

General-purpose rods 12, 23, 27, 40, 41
Glass-fibre 18, 19, 33
Greenstick fracture 18

Handles 35, 36, 49, 69

cork 36
double-handled 44
plastic 36
single-handled 44
wood-handled 36
Hollow-(fibre) glass 34

Leger rods 12, 23, 42
Line jamming 73
Line kink 70
Line snag 79
Line twist 70

Match rods 12, 23, 27, 28, 39, 41
Multiplying reels 44, 62, 71, 72, 76, 78

Nottingham reels 63

Overhead cast 87
Overrun (line) 64

Pike rods 15, 24, 27, 46
Plastic handles 36
Plastic reels 63
Playing a fish 67, 89, 90
Pole fishing 12, 25, 35, 46
alloy crook 47
elastic 47

Quivertips 42

Reels 59
automatic gearing 71

backplate 63
balancing rod and reel 61, 80
bale arms 69, 70
Bakelite 63
batting 64
'bird's nests' 61, 73
carbon-fibre 61
care 74
cases 74
centrepin 62, 63, 65, 72, 90
centrifugal braking 71
cleaning 74
closed-face 69
clutch 67
drag system 63, 67
drums 63, 71
filling with line 65, 70, 72, 79
fixed-spool 62, 66, 76, 90
for long-trotting 63
friction pads 71
gearing 68, 71
greasing 76, 79
line kink 70
line-snag 79
loading 65, 70, 72, 79
magnetic drag 71
multipliers (multiplying) 44, 62, 71, 72, 76, 78
Nottingham 63
oil drag retarders 71

oiling 76
overrun 64
plastic 63
retrieve 68
saddle 40
selection 60
skirted spool 67
spool 67, 71
stripping and cleaning
    76, 78
tension (knob) (nut)
    69
threadline, for
    trotting 66
wooden 63
Retrieve (reels) 68
Reverse taper 27
Roach poles (see Pole
    fishing)
Rod joints (sections) 17,
    33, 51
Rod rings 35, 37
    black chrome 37
    butt 38
    end 38
    satin chrome 37
    stainless steel 39
    stand-off 37
Rods
    action 29, 41, 42
    beachcasters 46
    blanks 47
    boron 19
    butts 26
    carbon fibre 19, 34

care of 36, 48, 49
choosing 39
cleaning 36, 49
combination rods 15
cord handles 36
cranked handled 44
double-handed 44
fast action 41
fast taper 26, 27, 29
'feel' 15
ferrules 33
fittings 35, 40, 41
for bait-casting 44
for spinning 24, 26, 35
general-purpose
    (float) rods 12,
    23, 27, 40, 41
glass-fibre 18, 19, 33
greenheart 17
greenstick fractures
    18
handles 35, 49
holdalls 50
hollow-cane 17
hollow-glass 34
joints 17, 33, 51
    female 33
    male 33
leger rods 23
length 23
maintenance 48
pike rods 25, 46
plastic handles 36
poles (roach poles)
    25, 46

quivertip 42
reel loading 72
reel saddle 40
repairs 51
reverse taper 27
rings 35, 37, 38
roach poles 25, 46
rod tubes 50
second-hand rods 17
selection 39
'set' 17
single-handed 35
sliding winch fittings
    40, 41
slow action 40
slow taper 29
soft action 29
spigots 34, 42, 51
spinning rods 24, 26,
    35, 44
split-cane 17
springtip 42
stiff action 29, 41, 42
swingtip 42
taper 26, 27, 29
test curve 31, 44, 45,
    46
tip 26
tip action 28, 30
whippings 52
whole cane 17
wood handles 36

Rod choosing 39
Rod repairs 51
Rod 'set'

Second-hand rods 17
Set (in rods) 17
Single-handed rods 35,
    44
Skirted spool 67
Sliding winch fittings
    40, 41
Spigots 34, 42, 51
Spinning rods 24, 26, 35,
    44
Split-cane 17
Spring balance 31
Springtip 42
Striking 21
Swingtip 42

Taper (rods) 26, 29
Test curve 31, 44, 45, 46
Threadline reels 66
Tip action 30
Tubes (for rods) 50

Underarm cast 86

Whippings (rods) 52
Whole cane 17